Wild Weather

Big Freeze

REVISED AND UPDATED

Heinemann
LIBRARY

Catherine Chambers

H **www.heinemann.co.uk/library**

Visit our website to find out more information about **Heinemann Library** books.

To order:

☎ Phone ++44 (0)1865 888112

🖷 Send a fax to ++44 (0)1865 314091

💻 Visit the Heinemann Bookshop at www.heinemann.co.uk/library to browse our catalogue and order online.

First published in Great Britain by Heinemann Library, Halley Court, Jordan Hill, Oxford OX2 8EJ, part of Harcourt Education. Heinemann is a registered trademark of Harcourt Education.

Editorial: Clare Lewis
Designed: Steve Mead and Q2A
Illustrations: Paul Bale
Picture Research: Tracy Cummins
Production: Julie Carter

Originated by Modern Age Repro
Printed and bound in China by South China Printing Company Limited

13 digit ISBN 978 0 431 15081 9 (hardback)
11 10 09 08 07
10 9 8 7 6 5 4 3 2 1

13 digit ISBN 978 0 431 15091 8 (paperback)
13 12 11 10 09 08
10 9 8 7 6 5 4 3 2 1

British Library Cataloguing in Publication Data

Chambers, Catherine
Wild Weather: Big Freeze. – 2nd Edition – Juvenile literature
551.5'253
A full catalogue record for this book is available from the British Library.

Acknowledgements

The Publishers would like to thank the following for permission to reproduce photographs: Ardea p19, Associated Press p26, Vanessa Berberian/Getty Images p20, Bryan and Cherry Alexander p27, Corbis pp5, 11, 17, 22, 24, 29, Imagebank p15, Photodisc pp4, 12, 13, 14, 28, Reuters p23, Robert Harding Picture Library p6, Tom Stewart/Corbis p21, Stone pp7, 18, 25, Telegraph Colour Library p9, Nik Wheeler/Corbis p16. Cover photograph of icicles hanging from a raspberry plant reproduced with permission of Gary W. Carter/Corbis.

The Publishers would like to thank Mark Rogers and the Met Office for their assistance with the preparation of this book.

Every effort has been made to contact copyright holders of any material reproduced in this book.
Any omissions will be rectified in subsequent printings if notice is given to the Publisher.

Any words appearing in the text in bold, **like this**, are explained in the Glossary.

Contents

What is a big freeze?

Some places on Earth are cold all the time. Others are warm all year round, but most places are cool in winter and warm in the summer.

■ *Mountainous areas are often cold.*

■ *This lake has frozen in the winter.*

Winter is usually about the same temperature every year. Sometimes it gets much colder than normal, even for winter. Rivers, lakes, and the ground may **freeze**. This is called a big freeze.

Where do big freezes happen?

The areas around the **North and South Poles** are cold all the time. Winter weather is normal there so it is not called a big **freeze**.

North Pole

Equator

South Pole

■ *It is always cold at the South Pole.*

■ *These oranges will be damaged by the cold weather.*

Florida in the United States is usually warm. When it suddenly gets cold there, people, plants, and animals may not be ready. They can be harmed by the cold. This is a big freeze.

What makes it so cold?

At the **North and South Poles**, the Sun's rays spread over a wider area. This makes the Sun's warmth weaker. In winter, these places **tilt** away from the Sun. The air and ground get really cold.

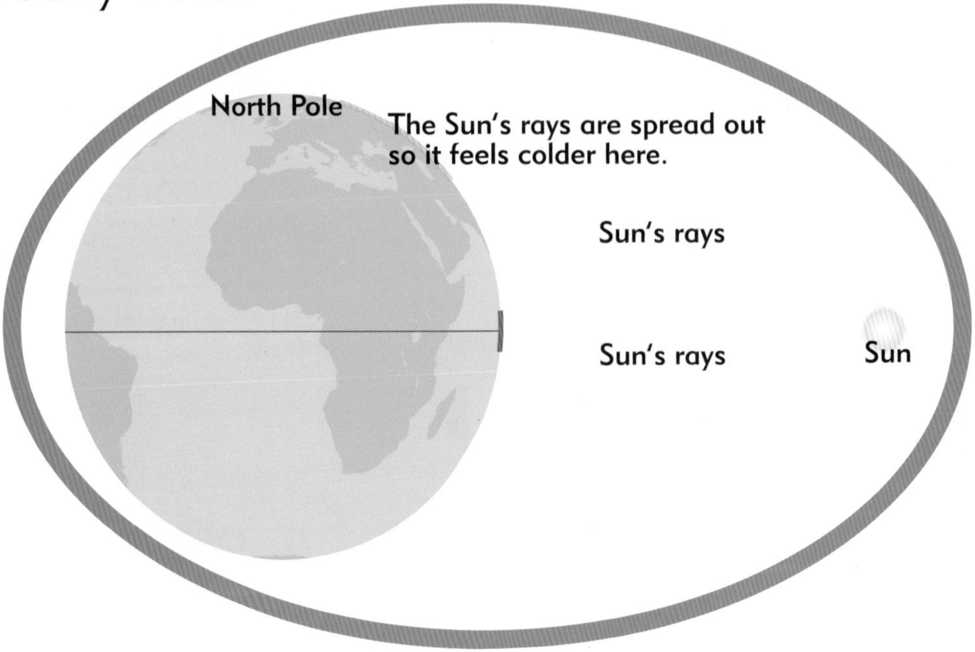

North Pole

The Sun's rays are spread out so it feels colder here.

Sun's rays

Sun's rays

Sun

■ *This diagram shows how the Sun heats the Earth.*

■ *Clear nights are very cold in the winter.*

Days are shorter during the winter so the Sun has less time to warm the Earth. Any heat in the ground rises high above the Earth when there are no clouds to stop it.

Why do big freezes happen?

The Earth is **surrounded** by moving **masses** of air. Some are warm and some are cold. A big **freeze** happens when a mass of cold air stays in one place for a long time.

■ *A big freeze can bring lots of snow.*

■ *Roads can be dangerous in a big freeze.*

These masses of cold air often come from around the **North and South Poles**, where it is cold all year round. Strong winds push the cold air to other places, bringing with them a big freeze.

What are big freezes like?

In a big **freeze**, the weather is even colder than normal winter weather. It is too cold for people to be outside for very long. They stay inside their heated houses.

■ *People wrap up warm if they are outside in a big freeze.*

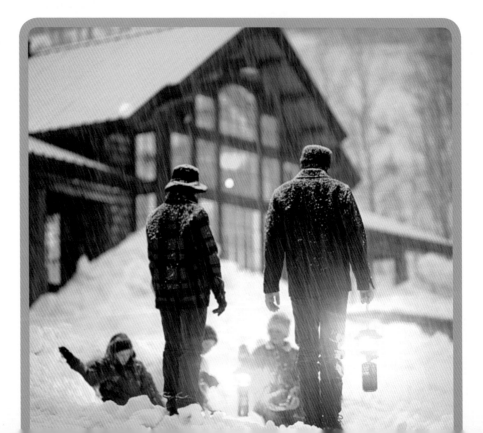

■ *Icy roads are difficult to drive on.*

Ice covers pavements and roads. People and **vehicles** slip and slide on it. Sometimes ice on roads is **invisible**. It is called **black ice** and is very dangerous.

Harmful freezes

It can be hard to travel in a big **freeze**. Ice can make roads slippery.

■ *Water has frozen around this boat. It cannot move.*

■ *This road has been flooded.*

Water freezes inside water pipes. The water **expands** when it freezes. It cracks the pipes. So water gushes out when the big freeze **thaws**. Houses and roads can be flooded.

Big freeze in Mongolia

This is the country of Mongolia. It lies in the middle of the **continent** called Asia. Warm, moist air from the sea cannot reach the middle of the continent.

■ *Mongolia is often cold.*

■ *In a big freeze, Mongolia is covered in snow.*

Most people in Mongolia are farmers. In one big **freeze** many cows and sheep died. They died because there was nothing to eat – all the grass was frozen.

Preparing for the big freeze

Some people stock up with food before a big **freeze** comes. Then they will not have to go outside to go shopping. Hospitals and chemists order plenty of extra medicines.

■ *People like to prepare for a big freeze by buying lots of food.*

■ *These trees are protected from the cold.*

A big freeze can kill **crops**. So farmers cover ground crops with **fleece**, material, or glass. They use heaters and wind machines to blow warm air on to fruit trees.

Coping with big freezes

When it is very cold, it is important to dress warmly. Wearing several layers of clothing under your coat will help keep you warm. Mittens, hats, and boots are important, too.

■ *These children are wearing warm clothes so they can play in the snow.*

■ *Eating a hot meal is a good idea when it is cold outside.*

It is best to stay inside during a big **freeze**. Getting enough to eat helps your body. Hot food and drinks are a tasty way to stay warm!

Big freeze in a hot country

India and Bangladesh are normally very hot countries. The type of clothes people wear help them to keep cool, not hot.

■ *Houses in India are not built to keep people warm.*

■ *It was very hard for people to keep warm when the cold weather came.*

In 2006 the weather in these countries was much colder than usual. Many people died because their clothes and houses could not protect them from the **freezing** weather.

Animals and plants in the big freeze

People who live in the Himalayan Mountains keep animals called yaks. Yaks are able to keep warm in the big **freezes** that can happen in the mountains.

■ *Yaks have hairy coats to keep them warm.*

■ *These strawberry plants are covered in ice.*

If big freezes come too early in the year, they can damage **crops**. Frost makes plants freeze and can stop them from growing.

To the rescue!

Cities in warm parts of the world may not have enough snowploughs and salt trucks to cope with a big **freeze**. They may have to borrow trucks from colder places.

■ *Snowploughs clear the roads so cars can get through.*

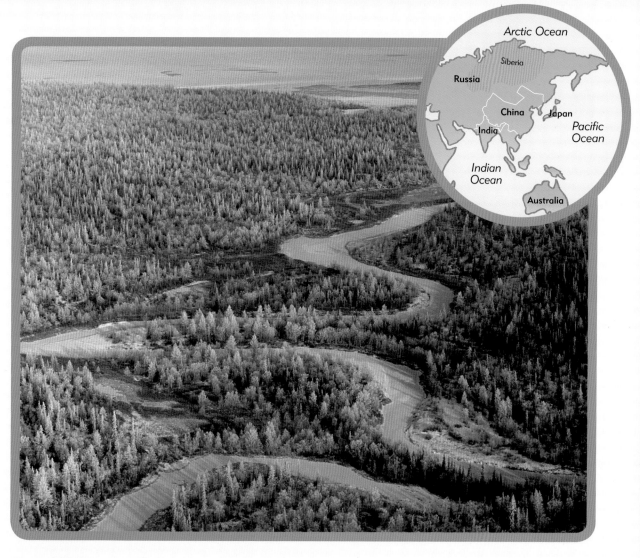

■ *In 2001, the River Lena froze over.*

Siberia in Russia is very cold in winter. In 2001 it was even colder than usual. Ice blocked the flow of the River Lena. Planes dropped bombs on the thick ice to stop the river from flooding.

Adapting to the big freeze

Most people in this country live in homes with central heating or fires. When a big **freeze** comes they can make their homes warmer.

■ *It is best to stay indoors with a warm fire when a big freeze comes.*

■ *A big freeze can be harmful to people who have no home.*

In many cities there are people without homes. They sleep outside on the street. For homeless people, a big freeze can be dangerous. It is important that they find food and **shelter**.

Fact file

◆ Ice on rivers and lakes is made of millions of frozen **crystals**. The crystals join together to make the ice look smooth.

◆ When it is really cold, the sea can **freeze**. Almost 300 years ago the King of Sweden led his army across the frozen sea to attack Denmark. Unfortunately the ice melted before they reached the other side.

Glossary

black ice thin layer of clear ice –
it looks black because the road
can be seen through it

continent huge mass of land that
has many different countries
on it

crops plants grown for food

crystals small shapes of
frozen water

expands gets bigger

fleece furry material

freeze change into ice or a solid

invisible cannot be seen

mass amount of something

North and South Poles end points
of a line around which the Earth
spins. The North and South Poles
are very cold.

shelter safe, warm place

surrounded all around,
everywhere

thaws melts

tilt moves slightly to one side

vehicles forms of transport. Cars,
buses, and trucks are all vehicles.

More books to read

Nature's Patterns: *Weather Patterns*, Monica Hughes (Heinemann Library, 2005).

The Weather: *Snow*, Terry Jennings (Chrysalis Children's Books, 2004)

Index